Practical
Vegetarian

p^3

This is a P³ Publishing Book
This edition published in 2004

P³ Publishing
Queen Street House
4 Queen Street
Bath BA1 1HE, UK

ISBN: 1-40543-284-5

Printed in China

NOTE

Cup measurements in this book are for American cups.
This book also uses imperial and metric measurements. Follow the same units
of measurement throughout; do not mix imperial and metric.
All spoon measurements are level: teaspoons are assumed to be 5 ml, and
tablespoons are assumed to be 15 ml. Unless otherwise stated,
milk is assumed to be whole milk, eggs and individual vegetables such as potatoes
are medium, and pepper is freshly ground black pepper.

The nutritional information provided for each recipe is per serving or per person.
Optional ingredients, variations, or serving suggestions have
not been included in the calculations. The times given for each recipe are an approximate
guide only because the preparation times may differ according to the techniques used by
different people and the cooking times may vary as a result of the type of oven used.

Recipes using raw or very lightly cooked eggs should be
avoided by infants, the elderly, pregnant women, convalescents,
and anyone suffering from an illness.

Contents

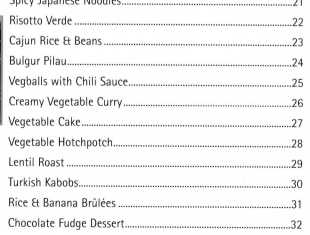

Introduction

Fruit and vegetables, which are natural sources of vitamins and minerals, form the basis of a huge variety of meals. These foods offer a multitude of different colors and variety of tastes which, when combined with herbs and spices, create an explosion of sumptuous flavors. Due to the enormous variety of foods available on the vegetarian menu, vegetarian cooking is now extremely popular with meat-eaters, vegetarians, and vegans alike. This book has combined the most traditional vegetarian dishes with new recipes, which together offer some unique and exciting flavors and textures. From pâtés or bhajias as appetizers, stuffed vegetables and noodles as entrées, to a delicious chocolate fudge dessert or rice and banana brûlées for desserts, this collection of recipes covers all areas of vegetarian cuisine.

Tasty vegetarian food

Vegetarian food has come a long way since the nut cutlet. Its growing popularity is due, at least in part, to the diverse range of influences—from Asia and North Africa, to Italy and Mexico—which have introduced to us  a whole new range of exciting ingredients enabling us to make delicious recipes from around the world. A wide variety of exotic foods can now easily be obtained in local supermarkets. These offer novel textures and flavors, making vegetarian cooking more interesting than ever. Try Risotto Verde or Warm Goat-Cheese Salad, or why not enjoy a delicious Spanish Tortilla or Turkish Kabobs?

Healthy eating

 Many people turn to vegetarian food because it is so healthy. Fruit and vegetables are naturally fat-free and provide plenty of fiber, carbohydrates, vitamins, and minerals. Each particular food has different nutritional benefits and these should be kept in mind when combining various ingredients to ensure a balanced diet.

In varying degrees, fruit and vegetables contain calcium, iron, and phosphorus, all of which are important for healthy living. Furthermore, fruit and vegetables are great sources of vitamin A, which is found in green, yellow, and orange vegetables, particularly in carrots. Leafy vegetables are an excellent source of vitamin E. Vitamin C is present in many "fruit vegetables," such as bell peppers and tomatoes, and may also be found in the roots and leaves of other vegetables. Strict vegetarians should ensure that sufficient levels of protein are maintained in their diets. This is not difficult, however, because vegetables can be eaten with beans, cheeses, or nuts, which offer natural sources of protein.

Beans

Beans are extremely important to a vegetarian diet and can be found in many forms, from lentils and navy beans, to kidney beans and field peas. The nutritional benefits of beans include high levels of carbohydrates, vitamins—especially vitamin B—and iron, which is especially important for women and the elderly. Each of the different beans gives a different texture to your dish and all can be combined with a rich variety of flavors.

Worldwide, local gastronomies have had enormous influence on the methods of preparing, cooking, and serving different beans. From Massachusetts, the home

of the baked bean, or Mexico and the ubiquitous *frijoles* or refried beans, to the tasty lentil dal of India, each region has found an innovative way of spicing up their food. Eating meals that combine beans with grains ensures you achieve the complete daily protein intake required in a healthy diet, so, for example, it is an excellent idea to mop up a lentil soup with tasty whole-wheat bread. Recipes have been included in this book that show you how to combine different food groups to create a variety of flavorsome dishes. Choose from Cajun Rice and Beans, Vegballs with Chili Sauce, or Creamy Vegetable Curry, among others, for a completely balanced meal.

Choosing and cooking vegetables

With such a huge variety of vegetables on the market, it is important to choose and cook them in the correct way. When purchasing vegetables, make sure that they are neither damaged nor bruised. Leafy vegetables should look green, not yellow, and the leaves should not be slimy or wilting. Root vegetables should be firm with a dull and dry appearance. Fruits should have taut, shiny skins and be firm to the touch.

Preparing vegetables incorrectly can lead to a leaching of vitamins and loss of all-important nutrients. Many vegetables can be eaten raw but cooking often enhances the flavor and changes their texture. There are many different ways in which they can be prepared, some of which do not require fat. Broiling and grilling leave the food with a crisp outer coating while maintaining moist and tender interiors; braising and stewing involve cooking

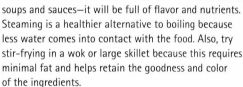

the dish very slowly using liquids—often the natural juices of the ingredients themselves—resulting in tender vegetables that retain all their nutrients, flavors, and aromas; boiling and poaching do not use any fat but can lead to loss of essential nutrients in the cooking water, which is then discarded.

If you do boil your vegetables, try to keep cooking times as short as possible in order to limit the loss of essential vitamins. And remember, the cooking water can be used afterward to make soups and sauces—it will be full of flavor and nutrients. Steaming is a healthier alternative to boiling because less water comes into contact with the food. Also, try stir-frying in a wok or large skillet because this requires minimal fat and helps retain the goodness and color of the ingredients.

Cooking vegetarian food for the first time

For those who have decided to convert to vegetarianism, or who are simply cooking meat-free food for the first time, there are several ingredients that should be avoided. In particular, gelatin, a protein used to thicken foods and which is used in many desserts, is made from collagen so a vegetarian substitute should be used instead. Also, many cheeses are made with animal derivatives: strict vegetarians should buy cheeses that have been certified by a recognized vegetarian association and have the association's symbol of approval on the label. Vegetarian cheeses are made with rennets of nonanimal origin, using microbial or fungal enzymes. When buying prepackaged ingredients, in particular sweet foods such as cookies, always check the ingredients to see if animal fats have been used. You should also be aware that some condiments may contain animal or fish products. For example, Worcestershire sauce is made using anchovies.

KEY		
	Simplicity level 1–3 (1 easiest, 3 slightly harder)	
	Preparation time	
	Cooking time	

Vegetable & Corn Chowder

This is a really filling soup, which should be served before a light entrée. It is easy to prepare and full of flavor.

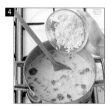

NUTRITIONAL INFORMATION

Calories 378	Sugars 20g
Protein 16g	Fat 13g
Carbohydrate . . .52g	Saturates 6g

15 mins   30 mins

SERVES 4

I N G R E D I E N T S

1 tbsp vegetable oil

1 red onion, diced

1 red bell pepper, seeded and diced

3 garlic cloves, crushed

1 large potato, diced

2 tbsp all-purpose flour

2½ cups milk

1¼ cups vegetable bouillon

1¾ oz/50 g broccoli florets

3 cups canned corn, drained weight

¾ cup colby cheese, grated

salt and pepper

1 tbsp chopped fresh cilantro, to garnish

1 Heat the oil in a large pan. Add the onion, bell pepper, garlic, and potato and then sauté over low heat, stirring frequently, for 2–3 minutes.

2 Stir in the flour and cook, stirring, for 30 seconds. Gradually stir in the milk and bouillon.

3 Add the broccoli florets and the corn. Bring the mixture to a boil, stirring constantly, then lower the heat and simmer for about 20 minutes, or until all the vegetables are tender.

4 Add ½ cup of the cheese and stir until it melts.

5 Season, then ladle the chowder into warm serving bowls. Garnish with the remaining cheese and the chopped fresh cilantro and serve.

Pumpkin Soup

This American classic has now become popular worldwide. When pumpkin is out of season, use butternut squash in its place.

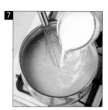

NUTRITIONAL INFORMATION

Calories 112   Sugars 7g
Protein . . . . .4g   Fat 7g
Carbohydrate . . . .8g   Saturates 2g

🥄 10 mins   🕐 30 mins

SERVES 6

I N G R E D I E N T S

about 2 lb 4 oz/1 kg pumpkin

3 tbsp butter or margarine

1 onion, thinly sliced

1 garlic clove, crushed

3¾ cups vegetable bouillon

½ tsp ground ginger

1 tbsp lemon juice

3–4 thinly pared strips of orange zest (optional)

1–2 bay leaves or 1 bouquet garni

1¼ cups milk

salt and pepper

TO GARNISH

4–6 tbsp light or heavy cream, plain yogurt, or fromage frais

snipped fresh chives

1 Peel the pumpkin, remove the seeds, and then cut the flesh into 1-inch/2.5-cm cubes.

2 Melt the butter or margarine in a large, heavy-bottomed pan.

3 Add the sliced onion and crushed garlic and cook over low heat, until soft but not colored.

4 Add the pumpkin and toss with the onion for 2–3 minutes.

5 Add the bouillon and bring to a boil over medium heat. Season to taste with salt and pepper and add the ginger, lemon juice, strips of orange zest, if using, and the bay leaves or bouquet garni. Cover and simmer over low heat for about 20 minutes, until the pumpkin is tender.

6 Discard the orange zest, if using, and the bay leaves or bouquet garni. Cool the soup slightly, then press through a strainer or process in a food processor until smooth. Pour into a clean pan.

7 Pour in the milk and reheat gently. Adjust the seasoning. Garnish with a swirl of cream, plain yogurt, or fromage frais, top with snipped chives, and serve.

Hummus & Garlic Toasts

Hummus is delicious spread on these flavorsome garlic toasts and makes a marvelous appetizer or snack.

NUTRITIONAL INFORMATION

Calories 731   Sugars 2g
Protein . . . . .22g   Fat 55g
Carbohydrate . . .39g   Saturates 8g

20 mins   3 mins

SERVES 4

I N G R E D I E N T S

14 oz/400 g canned garbanzo beans

juice of 1 large lemon

6 tbsp tahini (sesame seed paste)

2 tbsp olive oil

2 garlic cloves, finely chopped

salt and pepper

T O A S T S

1 ciabatta loaf, sliced

2 garlic cloves, finely chopped

1 tbsp chopped fresh cilantro

4 tbsp olive oil

T O   G A R N I S H

fresh cilantro, chopped

black olives

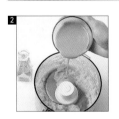  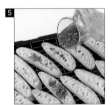

1 To make the hummus, first drain the garbanzo beans, reserving a little of the liquid. Put the garbanzo beans in a food processor and blend, gradually adding the reserved liquid and lemon juice. Blend well after each addition, until the mixture is smooth.

2 Pour in the tahini and then add all but 1 teaspoon of the olive oil. Add the garlic, season to taste, and blend again, until smooth.

3 Spoon the hummus into a serving dish. Drizzle the remaining olive oil over the top, and then garnish with the chopped fresh cilantro and the black olives. Let chill in the refrigerator while preparing the toasts.

4 Lay the slices of ciabatta on a broiler rack in a single layer.

5 Mix the garlic, cilantro, and olive oil together and drizzle over the bread slices. Cook the bread slices under a hot broiler for about 2–3 minutes, turning once, until golden brown. Serve hot with the hummus.

COOK'S TIP

Make the hummus 1 day in advance, and chill, covered, in the refrigerator until required. Garnish and serve.

Cheese, Garlic & Herb Pâté

This marvelous soft cheese pâté is fragrant with the aroma of fresh herbs and garlic. Serve with triangles of Melba toast for a perfect appetizer.

NUTRITIONAL INFORMATION

Calories 392	Sugars 1g	
Protein 17g	Fat 28g	
Carbohydrate ...18g	Saturates 18g	

  20 mins   10 mins

SERVES 4

INGREDIENTS

1 tbsp butter

1 garlic clove, crushed

3 scallions, finely chopped

generous ½ cup fullfat soft cheese

2 tbsp chopped mixed herbs, such as parsley, chives, marjoram, oregano, and basil

1¾ cups finely grated sharp colby cheese

pepper

4–6 slices of white bread from a medium-cut sliced loaf

mixed salad greens and cherry tomatoes, to serve

TO GARNISH

ground paprika

fresh herb sprigs

3 Add the colby cheese and work the mixture together to form a stiff paste. Cover and chill, until ready to serve.

4 To make the Melba toast, toast the slices of bread on both sides, then cut off the crusts. Using a sharp bread knife, cut through the slices horizontally to make very thin slices. Cut into triangles and then lightly broil the untoasted sides, until golden.

5 Arrange the mixed salad greens on 4 serving plates with the cherry tomatoes. Pile the cheese pâté on top and sprinkle with a little paprika. Garnish with sprigs of fresh herbs and serve with the Melba toast.

  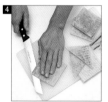

1 Melt the butter in a small skillet and gently cook the garlic and scallions together for 3–4 minutes, until softened. Let cool.

2 Beat the soft cheese in a large mixing bowl until smooth, then add the garlic and scallions. Stir in the herbs and mix well.

Vegetable Fritters

These mixed vegetable fritters are coated in a light batter and deep-fried until golden. They are ideal with the sweet-and-sour dipping sauce.

NUTRITIONAL INFORMATION

Calories 479   Sugars 18g
Protein ....8g   Fat 32g
Carbohydrate ...42g   Saturates 5g

🍲 20 mins   🕐 20 mins

SERVES 4

I N G R E D I E N T S

¾ cup whole-wheat flour

pinch of cayenne pepper

4 tsp olive oil

¾ cup cold water

3½ oz/100 g broccoli florets

3½ oz/100 g cauliflower florets

1¾ oz/50 g snow peas

1 large carrot, cut into batons

1 red bell pepper, seeded and sliced

2 egg whites, beaten

oil, for deep-frying

salt

S A U C E

⅔ cup pineapple juice

⅔ cup vegetable bouillon

2 tbsp white wine vinegar

2 tbsp light brown sugar

2 tsp cornstarch

2 scallions, chopped

1 Sift the flour and a pinch of salt into a mixing bowl and add the cayenne pepper. Make a well in the center and gradually beat in the oil and cold water to make a smooth batter.

2 Cook the vegetables in boiling water for 5 minutes and drain well.

3 Whisk the egg whites until they form stiff peaks and gently fold them into the flour batter.

4 Dip the vegetables into the batter, turning to coat well. Drain off any excess batter. Pour the oil for deep-frying into a deep fryer and heat to 350°F/180°C, or until a cube of bread browns in about 30 seconds. Cook the coated vegetables, in batches, for 1–2 minutes, until golden. Remove from the oil with a slotted spoon and drain on paper towels.

5 Place all of the sauce ingredients in a pan and bring to a boil, stirring, until thickened and clear. Serve with the fritters.

Mixed Bhajias

These small bhajias are often served as accompaniments to a main meal, but they are delicious as an appetizer with a small salad and yogurt sauce.

NUTRITIONAL INFORMATION

Calories 414	Sugars 7g	
Protein 9g	Fat 26g	
Carbohydrate . . .38g	Saturates 3g	

25 mins   30 mins

SERVES 4

INGREDIENTS

1¼ cups gram flour

1 tsp baking soda

2 tsp ground coriander

1 tsp garam masala

1½ tsp turmeric

1½ tsp chili powder

2 tbsp chopped fresh cilantro

1 small onion, halved and sliced

1 small leek, sliced

3½ oz/100 g cooked cauliflower

½–¾ cup cold water

vegetable oil, for deep-frying

salt and pepper

YOGURT SAUCE

⅔ cup plain yogurt

2 tbsp chopped fresh mint

½ tsp turmeric

1 garlic clove, crushed

sprig of fresh mint

  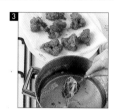

1 Sift the flour, baking soda, and a pinch of salt into a mixing bowl. Add the spices and the chopped fresh cilantro. Mix thoroughly.

2 Divide the mixture into 3 portions and place in separate bowls. Stir the onion into one bowl, the leek into the second bowl, and the cauliflower into the third bowl. Add 3–4 tbsp of water to each bowl, season, and mix the contents of each to form a smooth paste.

3 Pour the oil for deep-frying into a deep fryer and heat to 350°F/180°C, or until a cube of bread browns in 30 seconds.

Using 2 dessertspoons, form the mixture into balls and cook them in batches in the oil for 3–4 minutes, until browned. Remove with a slotted spoon and drain well on absorbent paper towels. Keep the bhajias warm in the oven while cooking in batches.

4 Mix all of the sauce ingredients together and pour into a small serving bowl. Top with a mint sprig and serve with the warm bhajias.

Corn & Potato Fritters

An ideal supper dish for two, or for one if you halve the quantities. You can use the remaining corn in another recipe.

NUTRITIONAL INFORMATION

Calories ....639 Sugars 17g
Protein ....28g Fat 31g
Carbohydrate ...65g Saturates 9g

20 mins   20 mins

SERVES 2

INGREDIENTS

2 tbsp oil

1 small onion, thinly sliced

1 garlic clove, crushed

12 oz/350 g potatoes

7 oz/200 g canned corn, drained

½ tsp dried oregano

1 egg, beaten

generous ½ cup grated Edam or Gouda cheese

2–4 eggs

2–4 tomatoes, sliced

salt and pepper

sprigs of fresh parsley, to garnish

1 Heat 1 tablespoon of the oil in a nonstick skillet. Add the onion and garlic and cook very gently, stirring frequently, until soft but only lightly colored. Remove from the heat.

2 Coarsely grate the potatoes into a bowl and mix in the corn, oregano, beaten egg, and salt and pepper to taste. Add the cooked onion.

3 Heat the remaining oil in the skillet. Divide the potato mixture in half and add to the pan to make 2 oval-shaped cakes, levelling and shaping the cakes with a spatula.

4 Cook the fritters over low heat for about 10 minutes, until golden brown underneath and almost cooked through, keeping them tidily in shape with the spatula and loosening them so that they do not stick to the bottom to the pan.

5 Sprinkle each potato fritter with the grated cheese and place under a preheated moderately-hot broiler, until golden brown.

6 Meanwhile, poach 1 or 2 eggs for each person, until just cooked. Transfer the fritters to warmed plates and top with the eggs and sliced tomatoes. Garnish with parsley and serve at once.

Mexican Salad

This is a colorful salad with a Mexican theme, using beans, tomatoes, and avocado. The chili dressing adds a little kick.

NUTRITIONAL INFORMATION

Calories . . . . . . .307 Sugars 7g
Protein . . . . .5g Fat 26g
Carbohydrate . . .13g Saturates 5g

  10–15 mins   0 mins

SERVES 4

I N G R E D I E N T S

lollo rosso lettuce

2 ripe avocados

2 tsp lemon juice

4 medium tomatoes

1 onion

2 cups canned mixed beans, drained

D R E S S I N G

4 tbsp olive oil

dash of chili oil

2 tbsp garlic wine vinegar

pinch of superfine sugar

pinch of chili powder

1 tbsp chopped fresh parsley

COOK'S TIP

The lemon juice is sprinkled onto the avocados to prevent discoloration when in contact with the air. For this reason, the salad should be prepared, assembled, and served quite quickly.

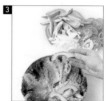

1 Line a large serving bowl with the lollo rosso lettuce.

2 Using a sharp knife, cut the avocados in half and remove the pits. Thinly slice the flesh and immediately sprinkle with the lemon juice.

3 Thinly slice the tomatoes and onion and push the onion out into rings. Arrange the avocado, tomatoes, and onion around the salad bowl, leaving a space in the center.

4 Spoon the beans into the center of the salad. Put all of the dressing ingredients in a bowl and whisk together. Pour the dressing over the salad and serve.

Warm Goat Cheese Salad

This delicious salad combines soft goat cheese with walnut halves, served on a bed of mixed salad greens.

NUTRITIONAL INFORMATION

Calories	408	Sugars	.........8g
Protein	.........9g	Fat	..........38g
Carbohydrate	....8g	Saturates	.......8g

5 mins   5 mins

SERVES 4

INGREDIENTS

¾ cup walnut halves

mixed salad greens

4½ oz/125 g soft goat cheese

snipped fresh chives, to garnish

DRESSING

6 tbsp walnut oil

3 tbsp white wine vinegar

1 tbsp clear honey

1 tsp Dijon mustard

pinch of ground ginger

salt and pepper

1 To make the dressing, whisk together the walnut oil, wine vinegar, honey, mustard, and ginger in a small pan. Season to taste with salt and pepper.

2 Heat the dressing gently, stirring occasionally, until warm. Add the walnut halves and continue to heat for 3–4 minutes.

3 Arrange the salad greens on 4 serving plates and place spoonfuls of goat cheese on top. Using a slotted spoon, lift the walnut halves from the dressing and scatter them over the salad.

4 Transfer the warm dressing to a small pitcher. Arrange the chives on the salad and serve with the dressing.

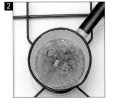 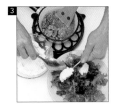 

VARIATION

You could also use a ewe's milk cheese, such as feta, in this recipe for a sharper flavor.

Spanish Tortilla

This classic Spanish dish is often served as part of a tapas selection.
A variety of cooked vegetables can be added to this recipe.

NUTRITIONAL INFORMATION

Calories	430	Sugars	.........6g
Protein	........16g	Fat	..........20g
Carbohydrate	...50g	Saturates	.......4g

10 mins   35 mins

SERVES 4

I N G R E D I E N T S

2 lb 4 oz/1 kg waxy potatoes, thinly sliced

4 tbsp vegetable oil

1 onion, sliced

2 garlic cloves, crushed

1 green bell pepper, seeded and diced

2 tomatoes, seeded and chopped

2½ tbsp canned corn, drained

6 large eggs, beaten

2 tbsp chopped fresh parsley

salt and pepper

1 Parboil the potatoes in a pan of lightly salted boiling water for 5 minutes. Drain well.

2 Heat the vegetable oil in a large skillet with a heatproof handle. Add

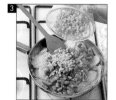

the potatoes and onion and then sauté over low heat, stirring constantly, for 5 minutes, until the potatoes have browned.

3 Add the garlic, green bell pepper, tomatoes, and corn, and mix well.

4 Pour in the eggs and add the parsley. Season to taste with salt and pepper. Cook the tortilla for 10–12 minutes, until the underside is cooked through.

5 Remove the skillet from the heat and continue to cook the tortilla under a preheated medium broiler for 5–7 minutes, or until the tortilla is set and the top is golden brown.

6 Cut the tortilla into wedges or cubes, depending on your preference, and transfer to serving dishes. Serve with salad. In Spain tortillas are served hot, cold, or warm.

COOK'S TIP

Ensure that the handle of your pan is heatproof before placing it under the broiler and be sure to use an oven mitt when removing it because it will be very hot.

Refried Beans with Tortillas

Refried beans are a classic Mexican dish and are usually served as an accompaniment. They are also delicious served with warm tortillas.

NUTRITIONAL INFORMATION

Calories 519	Sugars 14g	
Protein 25g	Fat 28g	
Carbohydrate . . .44g	Saturates 9g	

 15 mins   15 mins

SERVES 4

I N G R E D I E N T S

2 tbsp olive oil

1 onion, finely chopped

3 garlic cloves, finely chopped

1 green chile, seeded and chopped

14 oz/400 g canned red kidney beans, drained

14 oz/400 g canned pinto beans, drained

2 tbsp chopped fresh cilantro

⅔ cup vegetable bouillon

8 wheat tortillas

¼ cup grated colby cheese

salt and pepper

RELISH

4 scallions, chopped

1 red onion, chopped

1 green chile, seeded and chopped

1 tbsp garlic wine vinegar

1 tsp superfine sugar

1 tomato, chopped

1 Heat the oil in a large skillet. Add the chopped onion and sauté for 3–5 minutes. Add the garlic and chile and cook for 1 minute.

2 Put all the beans into a bowl, mash with a potato masher, then stir into the pan with the cilantro.

3 Stir in the bouillon. Cook the beans, stirring, for 5 minutes, until soft.

4 Place the tortillas on a cookie sheet and heat through in a warm oven for 1–2 minutes.

5 To make the relish, put all of the ingredients into a bowl and mix together well.

6 Spoon the beans into serving dishes and top with the cheese. Season well. Roll the warm tortillas and serve with the relish and beans.

Mixed Bean Pan-Fry

Fresh green beans have a marvelous flavor that is hard to beat. If you cannot find fresh beans, use frozen beans that have been thawed instead.

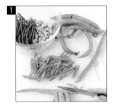  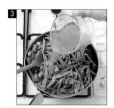

NUTRITIONAL INFORMATION

Calories 179   Sugars 4g
Protein ....10g   Fat 11g
Carbohydrate ...10g   Saturates 1g

 10 mins   15 mins

SERVES 4

I N G R E D I E N T S

12 oz/350 g mixed fresh beans, such as green beans and fava beans

2 tbsp vegetable oil

2 garlic cloves, crushed

1 red onion, halved and sliced

8 oz/225 g firm marinated bean curd, diced

1 tbsp lemon juice

½ tsp ground turmeric

1 tsp ground allspice

⅔ cup vegetable bouillon

2 tsp sesame seeds

1 Trim and chop the green beans and set aside until required.

2 Heat the oil in a medium skillet. Add the garlic and onion and cook over low heat, stirring frequently, for 2 minutes. Add the bean curd and then cook, stirring occasionally, for another 2–3 minutes, until just beginning to turn golden brown.

3 Add the chopped green beans and the fava beans. Stir in the lemon juice, ground turmeric, ground allspice, and vegetable bouillon and bring to a boil over medium heat.

4 Lower the heat and simmer for about 5–7 minutes, or until the beans are tender. Sprinkle with sesame seeds and serve immediately.

VARIATION
Use smoked bean curd instead of marinated bean curd for an alternative and distinctive flavor.

Three-Cheese Fondue

A hot cheese dip made from three different cheeses can be prepared easily and with guaranteed success in a microwave oven.

NUTRITIONAL INFORMATION

Calories 565	Sugars 1g
Protein 29g	Fat 38g
Carbohydrate . . .15g	Saturates 24g

 15 mins   🕙 10 mins

SERVES 4

I N G R E D I E N T S

1 garlic clove

1¼ cups dry white wine

2½ cups grated mild colby cheese

1¼ cups grated Swiss cheese

1¼ cups grated mozzarella cheese

2 tbsp cornstarch

pepper

T O   S E R V E

French bread

fresh vegetables, such as zucchini, mushrooms, baby corn cobs, and cauliflower

1 Bruise the garlic by placing the flat side of a knife on top and pressing down with the heel of your hand.

2 Rub the garlic around the inside of a large, microwave-proof bowl. Discard the garlic.

3 Pour the wine into the bowl and heat, uncovered, on HIGH power for 3–4 minutes, until hot but not boiling.

4 Gradually add the colby and Swiss cheeses, stirring well after each addition, then add the mozzarella. Stir until completely melted.

5 Mix the cornstarch with a little water to form a smooth paste and stir it into the cheese mixture. Season to taste with pepper.

6 Cover the bowl and cook on MEDIUM power for 6 minutes, stirring twice during cooking, until the sauce is smooth.

7 Cut the French bread into cubes and the vegetables into batons, slices, or florets. To serve, keep the fondue warm over a spirit lamp or burner, or reheat as necessary in the microwave oven. Dip in cubes of French bread and the batons, slices, or florets of vegetables.

COOK'S TIP

Make sure you add the cheese to the wine gradually, mixing well between each addition, otherwise the mixture might curdle.

Stuffed Globe Artichokes

This imaginative recipe for artichokes stuffed with nuts, tomatoes, olives, and mushrooms has been adapted for the microwave oven.

NUTRITIONAL INFORMATION

Calories 248   Sugars 8g
Protein ....5g   Fat 19g
Carbohydrate ...16g   Saturates 2g

🍲 30 mins   🕐 25 mins

SERVES 4

INGREDIENTS

4 globe artichokes

½ cup water

4 tbsp lemon juice

1 onion, chopped

1 garlic clove, crushed

2 tbsp olive oil

3 cups button mushrooms, chopped

½ cup pitted black olives, sliced

¼ cup sun-dried tomatoes in oil, drained (oil reserved) and chopped

1 tbsp chopped fresh basil

generous 1 cup fresh white bread crumbs

scant ¼ cup pine nuts, toasted

salt and pepper

a leaf pulls away easily from the bottom. Let stand, covered, for 3 minutes before draining. Turn the artichokes upside down and let cool. Repeat this process to cook the remaining artichokes.

2 Place the onion, garlic, and oil in a microwave-proof bowl. Cover and cook on HIGH power for 2 minutes, stirring once. Add the mushrooms, olives, and sun-dried tomatoes. Cover and cook on HIGH power for 2 minutes.

3 Stir in the basil, bread crumbs, and pine nuts. Season to taste with salt and pepper.

4 Turn the artichokes the right way up and carefully pull the leaves apart. Remove the purple-tipped central leaves. Using a teaspoon, scrape out the hairy chokes and discard.

5 Divide the stuffing into 4 equal portions and spoon into the center of each artichoke. Push the leaves back around the stuffing.

6 Arrange in a shallow dish and drizzle over a little reserved oil from the jar of sun-dried tomatoes. Cook on HIGH power for 7–8 minutes to reheat, turning the artichokes around halfway through.

1 Cut off the stalks and lower leaves of the artichokes. Snip off the leaf tips with scissors. Place 2 artichokes in a large, microwave-proof bowl with half the water and half the lemon juice. Cover and cook on HIGH power for 10 minutes, turning the artichokes over halfway through, until

Falafel

These are a very tasty, well-known Middle Eastern dish of small garbanzo bean balls, spiced and deep-fried.

NUTRITIONAL INFORMATION

Calories 491	Sugars 3g
Protein 15g	Fat 30g
Carbohydrate . . .43g	Saturates 3g

25 mins   10–15 mins

SERVES 4

I N G R E D I E N T S

6 cups canned garbanzo beans, drained

1 red onion, chopped

3 garlic cloves, crushed

3½ oz/100 g whole-wheat bread

2 small red chiles

1 tsp ground cumin

1 tsp ground coriander

½ tsp ground turmeric

1 tbsp chopped fresh cilantro, plus extra to garnish

1 egg, beaten

2 cups fresh whole-wheat bread crumbs

vegetable oil, for deep-frying

salt and pepper

TO SERVE

tomato and cucumber salad

lemon wedges

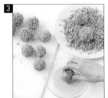

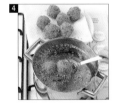

1 Put the garbanzo beans, onion, garlic, bread, chiles, spices, and chopped cilantro in a food processor and process for 30 seconds. Stir and season to taste with salt and pepper.

2 Remove the mixture from the food processor and use your hands to shape it into walnut-size balls.

3 Place the beaten egg in a shallow bowl and scatter the whole-wheat bread crumbs over a plate. Dip the balls first into the egg to coat them and then roll them in the bread crumbs, shaking off any excess.

4 Heat the oil for deep-frying to 350°F/180°C, or until a cube of bread browns in 30 seconds. Cook the falafel, in batches if necessary, for 2–3 minutes, until crisp and browned. Remove them from the oil with a slotted spoon and then dry them on absorbent paper towels. Garnish with the remaining cilantro and serve with a tomato and cucumber salad and lemon wedges.

Spicy Japanese Noodles

These noodles are highly spiced with chili and flavored with sesame seeds for a nutty taste that is a true delight.

NUTRITIONAL INFORMATION

Calories 381   Sugars 12g
Protein . . . . .11g   Fat 13g
Carbohydrate . . .59g   Saturates 2g

 5 mins   15 mins

SERVES 4

INGREDIENTS

1 lb 2 oz/500 g fresh Japanese noodles

1 tbsp sesame oil

1 tbsp sesame seeds

1 tbsp sunflower oil

1 red onion, sliced

3½ oz/100 g snow peas

2 carrots, thinly sliced

12 oz/350 g white cabbage, shredded

3 tbsp sweet chili sauce

2 scallions, sliced, to garnish

1 Bring a large pan of water to a boil. Add the Japanese noodles to the pan and cook for 2–3 minutes. Drain the noodles thoroughly.

2 Toss the noodles with the sesame oil and sesame seeds.

3 Heat the sunflower oil in a large, preheated wok or skillet.

4 Add the onion slices, snow peas, carrot slices, and shredded cabbage to the wok and cook for about 5 minutes.

5 Add the sweet chili sauce to the wok and cook, stirring occasionally, for another 2 minutes.

6 Add the sesame noodles to the wok, toss well to combine, and heat through for another 2–3 minutes. (You may also cook and serve the noodles separately, if you desire.)

7 Transfer the Japanese noodles and spicy vegetables to warm serving bowls and garnish with sliced scallions. Serve immediately.

COOK'S TIP

If fresh Japanese noodles are difficult to obtain, use dried rice noodles or thin egg noodles instead.

Risotto Verde

Baby spinach and fresh herbs are the basis of this colorful, refreshing, and summery risotto.

NUTRITIONAL INFORMATION

Calories 374	Sugars 5g	
Protein 10g	Fat 9g	
Carbohydrate ...55g	Saturates 2g	

 5 mins   🕐 40 mins

SERVES 4

INGREDIENTS

7½ cups vegetable bouillon

2 tbsp olive oil

2 garlic cloves, crushed

2 leeks, shredded

2 cups arborio rice

1¼ cups dry white wine

4 tbsp chopped fresh mixed herbs

8 oz/225 g baby spinach

3 tbsp lowfat plain yogurt

salt and pepper

shredded leek, to garnish

1 Pour the bouillon into a large pan and bring to a boil. Lower the heat to a simmer.

2 Meanwhile, heat the oil in a separate pan and cook the garlic and leeks, stirring occasionally, for 2–3 minutes, until softened but not browned.

3 Stir in the rice and cook, stirring constantly, until translucent and well coated with oil.

4 Pour in half of the wine and a little of the hot bouillon; it will bubble and steam rapidly. Cook over gentle heat, until all of the liquid has been absorbed.

5 Gradually stir in the remaining bouillon and wine and then cook over low heat for 25 minutes, or until the rice is creamy.

6 Stir in the chopped mixed herbs and baby spinach, season to taste with salt and pepper, and cook for another 2 minutes. Stir in the plain yogurt, garnish with the shredded leek, and serve the risotto immediately.

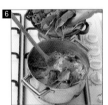

COOK'S TIP

Do not hurry the process of cooking the risotto because the rice must absorb the liquid slowly in order for it to reach the correct consistency.

Cajun Rice & Beans

Cajun spices add a delicious flavor to this appealing and colorful rice and red kidney bean salad.

NUTRITIONAL INFORMATION

Calories . . . . .336 Sugars 8g
Protein . . . . .7g Fat 13g
Carbohydrate . . .51g Saturates 2g

10 mins   15 mins

SERVES 4

I N G R E D I E N T S

scant 1 cup long-grain rice

4 tbsp olive oil

1 small green bell pepper, seeded
  and chopped

1 small red bell pepper, seeded
  and chopped

1 onion, finely chopped

1 small red or green chile, seeded and
  finely chopped

2 tomatoes, chopped

½ cup canned red kidney beans, rinsed
  and drained

1 tbsp chopped fresh basil

2 tsp chopped fresh thyme

1 tsp Cajun spice

salt and pepper

fresh basil leaves, to garnish

1 Cook the rice in plenty of boiling, lightly salted water for about 12 minutes, until just tender. Rinse with cold water and drain well.

2 Meanwhile, heat the olive oil in a skillet and cook the green and red bell peppers and the onion gently for about 5 minutes, until softened.

3 Add the chile and tomatoes and cook for another 2 minutes.

4 Add the vegetable mixture and red kidney beans to the rice. Stir well to combine thoroughly.

5 Stir the chopped herbs and Cajun spice into the rice mixture. Season to taste with salt and pepper, and serve garnished with basil leaves.

Bulgur Pilau

Bulgur is very easy to use and, as well as being full of nutrients, it has a distinctive nutty flavor. It makes a delicious alternative to rice.

NUTRITIONAL INFORMATION

Calories	637	Sugars	........25g
Protein	.........16g	Fat	..........26g
Carbohydrate	...90g	Saturates	......11g

 15 mins   35–40 mins

SERVES 4

INGREDIENTS

6 tbsp butter or margarine

1 red onion, halved and sliced

2 garlic cloves, crushed

2 cups bulgur

6 oz/175 g tomatoes, seeded and chopped

½ cup baby corn cobs, halved lengthwise

3 oz/85 g small broccoli florets

3¾ cups vegetable bouillon

2 tbsp honey

⅓ cup golden raisins

½ cup pine nuts

½ tsp ground cinnamon

½ tsp ground cumin

salt and pepper

thinly sliced scallions, to garnish

COOK'S TIP

The dish is left to stand for 10 minutes so that the bulgur can finish cooking and the flavors of the ingredients will mingle.

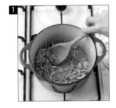  

1 Melt the butter or margarine in a large, flameproof casserole over medium heat. Add the onion and garlic. Cook, stirring occasionally, for 2–3 minutes, until softened but not browned.

2 Add the bulgur, tomatoes, corn cobs, broccoli florets, and vegetable bouillon and bring to a boil. Lower the heat, cover, and simmer gently, stirring occasionally, for 15–20 minutes.

3 Stir in the honey, golden raisins, pine nuts, ground cinnamon, and cumin, and season with salt and pepper to taste. Mix together well. Remove the casserole from the heat and set aside, covered, for 10 minutes.

4 Spoon the bulgur pilau into a warmed serving dish. Garnish the pilau with the thinly sliced scallions and then serve the dish immediately.

Vegballs with Chili Sauce

These tasty, nutty morsels are delicious served with a fiery, tangy sauce that counteracts the richness of the peanuts.

NUTRITIONAL INFORMATION

Calories	615	Sugars	. . . . .13g
Protein	. . . . .23g	Fat	. . . . .43g
Carbohydrate	. . .37g	Saturates	. . . . . . .8g

 25 mins   30 mins

SERVES 4

INGREDIENTS

3 tbsp peanut oil

1 onion, finely chopped

1 celery stalk, chopped

1 tsp dried mixed herbs

scant 2 cups roasted unsalted
   peanuts, ground

1 cup canned garbanzo beans, drained
   and mashed

1 tsp yeast extract

1 cup fresh whole-wheat bread crumbs

1 egg yolk

scant ¼ cup all-purpose flour

strips of fresh red chile, to garnish

HOT CHILI SAUCE

2 tsp peanut oil

1 large red chile, seeded and finely chopped

2 scallions, finely chopped

2 tbsp red wine vinegar

7 oz/200 g canned chopped tomatoes

2 tbsp tomato paste

2 tsp superfine sugar

salt and pepper

TO SERVE

freshly cooked rice

fresh salad greens

1 Heat 1 tablespoon of the oil in a skillet and gently cook the onion and celery for 3–4 minutes, until softened but not browned.

2 Put the herbs, peanuts, garbanzo beans, yeast extract, bread crumbs, and egg yolk in a mixing bowl. Add the onion and celery and mix well.

3 Divide the mixture into 12 portions and roll into small balls. Coat all over with the flour.

4 Heat the remaining oil in a skillet. Add the garbanzo bean balls and cook over medium heat, turning frequently, for 15 minutes, until cooked through and golden. Drain on paper towels.

5 Meanwhile, make the hot chili sauce. Heat the oil in a small skillet an gently cook the chile and scallions for about 2–3 minutes. Stir in the remaining ingredients and season. Bring to a boil and simmer for 5 minutes.

6 Serve the garbanzo bean balls with the hot chili sauce, freshly cooked rice, and fresh salad greens.

Creamy Vegetable Curry

These vegetables are cooked in a mildly spiced curry sauce with yogurt and fresh cilantro stirred in just before serving.

NUTRITIONAL INFORMATION

Calories 423   Sugars 24g
Protein . . . . .16g   Fat 19g
Carbohydrate . . .50g   Saturates 7g

  20 mins  25 mins

SERVES 4

INGREDIENTS

2 tbsp sunflower oil

1 onion, sliced

2 tsp cumin seeds

2 tbsp ground coriander

1 tsp ground turmeric

2 tsp ground ginger

1 tsp chopped fresh red chile

2 garlic cloves, chopped

14 oz/400 g canned chopped tomatoes

3 tbsp ground coconut mixed with
   1¼ cups boiling water

1 small cauliflower, broken into florets

2 zucchini, sliced

2 carrots, sliced

1 potato, diced

14 oz/400 g canned garbanzo beans,
   drained and rinsed

⅔ cup thick plain yogurt

2 tbsp mango chutney

3 tbsp chopped fresh cilantro

salt and pepper

fresh herbs, to garnish

freshly cooked rice, to serve

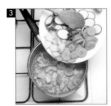

1 Heat the oil in a skillet and cook the onion until softened. Add the cumin, coriander, turmeric, ginger, chile, and garlic and cook for 1 minute.

2 Add the tomatoes and coconut mixture and mix well.

3 Add the cauliflower florets, zucchini, carrots, potato, and garbanzo beans, and season to taste with salt and pepper. Cover and simmer for 20 minutes, until the vegetables are tender.

4 Stir in the yogurt, mango chutney, and fresh cilantro and heat through gently, but do not boil. Transfer to a warm serving dish, garnish with fresh herbs, and serve with freshly cooked rice.

Vegetable Cake

This is a savory version of a cheesecake with a delicious layer of potatoes on the bottom. Use frozen mixed vegetables for the topping, if you prefer.

NUTRITIONAL INFORMATION

Calories	502	Sugars	.........8g
Protein	........16g	Fat	..........31g
Carbohydrate	...41g	Saturates	......14g

20 mins   45 mins

SERVES 4

I N G R E D I E N T S

2 tbsp vegetable oil, plus extra
 for brushing

4 large waxy potatoes, sliced

T O P P I N G

1 tbsp vegetable oil

1 leek, chopped

1 zucchini, grated

1 red bell pepper, seeded and diced

1 green bell pepper, seeded and diced

1 carrot, grated

2 tsp chopped fresh parsley

1 cup fullfat soft cheese

4 tbsp grated sharp cheese

2 eggs, beaten

salt and pepper

cooked leek, shredded, to garnish

crisp salad greens, to serve

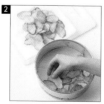

1 Brush an 8-inch/20-cm springform cake pan with oil.

2 To make the potato layer, heat the oil in a skillet. Cook the potato slices until softened and browned. Drain on paper towels and place in the bottom of the prepared cake pan.

3 To make the topping, heat the oil in a separate skillet. Add the leek and cook over low heat, stirring frequently, for 3–4 minutes, until softened.

4 Add the zucchini, bell peppers, carrot, and parsley to the skillet and cook over low heat for 5–7 minutes, or until the vegetables have softened.

5 Meanwhile, beat the cheeses and eggs together in a bowl. Stir in the vegetables and season to taste with salt and pepper. Spoon the mixture evenly over the potato in the cake pan.

6 Cook in a preheated oven, 375°F/190°C, for 20–25 minutes, until the cake is set.

7 Remove the vegetable cake from the pan, transfer to a warm serving plate, garnish with shredded leek, and serve with crisp salad greens.

Vegetable Hotchpotch

In this recipe, a variety of vegetables are arranged under a layer of potatoes, topped with cheese, and cooked until golden brown.

NUTRITIONAL INFORMATION

Calories 279   Sugars 12g
Protein .... 10g   Fat 11g
Carbohydrate ... 34g   Saturates 4g

25 mins   1 hour

SERVES 4

I N G R E D I E N T S

2 large potatoes, thinly sliced

2 tbsp vegetable oil

1 red onion, halved and sliced

1 leek, sliced

2 garlic cloves, crushed

1 carrot, cut into chunks

3½ oz/100 g broccoli florets

3½ oz/100 g cauliflower florets

2 small turnips, cut into fourths

1 tbsp all-purpose flour

3 cups vegetable bouillon

⅔ cup hard cider

1 eating apple, cored and sliced

2 tbsp chopped fresh sage

pinch of cayenne pepper

½ cup grated colby cheese

salt and pepper

1 Cook the potato slices in a pan of boiling water for 10 minutes. Drain thoroughly and reserve.

2 Heat the oil in a flameproof casserole. Add the onion, leek, and garlic and sauté, stirring occasionally, for 2–3 minutes. Add the remaining vegetables and cook, stirring constantly, for another 3–4 minutes.

3 Stir in the flour and cook for 1 minute. Gradually pour in the bouillon and hard cider and bring to a boil. Add the apple, sage, and cayenne pepper and season well. Remove from the heat and transfer the vegetables to an ovenproof dish.

4 Arrange the potato slices on top of the vegetable mixture and cover evenly.

5 Sprinkle the cheese on top of the potato slices and cook in a preheated oven, 375°F/190°C, for 30–35 minutes, or until the potato is golden brown and beginning to go crisp around the edges. Serve immediately.

Lentil Roast

The perfect dish to serve for Sunday lunch. Roasted vegetables make a succulent accompaniment.

NUTRITIONAL INFORMATION

Calories	400	Sugars	. . . . .2g
Protein	. . . . .26g	Fat	. . . . .20g
Carbohydrate	. . .32g	Saturates	. . . . . .10g

🄖 🄖

🕐 15 mins   🕑 1 hr 20 mins

SERVES 6

I N G R E D I E N T S

generous 1 cup red lentils

scant 2 cups vegetable bouillon

1 bay leaf

1 tbsp butter or margarine, softened

2 tbsp dried whole-wheat bread crumbs

generous 2 cups grated sharp colby cheese

1 leek, finely chopped

1⅔ cups finely chopped button mushrooms

1½ cups fresh whole-wheat bread crumbs

2 tbsp chopped fresh parsley

1 tbsp lemon juice

2 eggs, lightly beaten

salt and pepper

sprigs of fresh flatleaf parsley, to garnish

selection of roasted vegetables, to serve

1 Put the lentils, bouillon, and bay leaf in a pan. Bring to a boil, cover, and simmer gently for 15–20 minutes, until all the liquid is absorbed and the lentils have softened. Discard the bay leaf.

2 Line the bottom of a 2¼-lb/1-kg loaf pan with baking parchment. Grease with the butter or margarine and sprinkle with the dried bread crumbs.

3 Stir the cheese, leek, mushrooms, fresh bread crumbs, and chopped parsley into the lentils.

4 Bind the mixture together with the lemon juice and eggs. Season with salt and pepper. Spoon into the prepared loaf pan and smooth the top.

5 Bake in a preheated oven, 375°F/190°C, for about 1 hour, until golden.

6 Loosen the loaf with a spatula and turn out onto a warmed serving plate. Garnish with sprigs of parsley and serve sliced, with roasted vegetables.

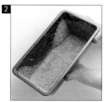

Turkish Kabobs

A spicy garbanzo bean sauce is served with colorful, grilled vegetable kabobs in this recipe—perfect for a lunch on a warm summer's day.

NUTRITIONAL INFORMATION

Calories	303	Sugars	........13g
Protein	.........13g	Fat	..........15g
Carbohydrate	...30g	Saturates	.......2g

 20 mins   🕐 20 mins

SERVES 4

I N G R E D I E N T S

1 eggplant

1 red bell pepper, seeded

1 green bell pepper, seeded

4 plum tomatoes

1 lemon, cut into wedges

8 small bay leaves

olive oil, for brushing

SAUCE

4 tbsp olive oil

3 garlic cloves, crushed

1 small onion, finely chopped

15 oz/425 g canned garbanzo beans, rinsed and drained

1¼ cups plain yogurt

1 tsp ground cumin

½ tsp chili powder

lemon juice

salt and pepper

1 To make the sauce, heat the olive oil in a small skillet. Add the garlic and chopped onion and cook over medium heat, stirring occasionally, for about 5 minutes, until the onion is softened and has turned golden brown.

2 Put the garbanzo beans and yogurt into a blender or food processor and add the cumin, chili powder, and onion mixture. Process for about 15 seconds, until smooth. Alternatively, mash the garbanzo beans with a potato masher and stir in the yogurt, ground cumin, chili powder, and onion mixture.

3 Scrape the mixture into a bowl and add lemon juice. Season with salt and pepper. Cover with plastic wrap and chill in the refrigerator, until ready to serve.

4 Cut the vegetables into large chunks and thread them alternately onto 4 skewers, placing a bay leaf and lemon wedge at both ends of each kabob.

5 Brush the kabobs with olive oil and cook them on a barbecue grill, turning frequently, for 5–8 minutes. Alternatively, cook under a preheated broiler. Heat the sauce and serve with the kabobs.

Rice & Banana Brûlées

Take a can of creamed rice, flavor it with orange rind, candied ginger, raisins, and sliced bananas and top with a brown sugar glaze.

NUTRITIONAL INFORMATION

Calories	509	Sugars	.......98g
Protein	.........9g	Fat	...........6g
Carbohydrate	...112g	Saturates	.......4g

5 mins   5 mins

SERVES 2

INGREDIENTS

14 oz/400 g canned creamed rice

grated rind of ½ orange

2 pieces of candied ginger, finely chopped

2 tsp ginger syrup from the jar of candied ginger

⅓ cup raisins

1–2 bananas

1–2 tsp lemon juice

4–5 tbsp raw brown sugar

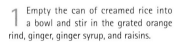

1 Empty the can of creamed rice into a bowl and stir in the grated orange rind, ginger, ginger syrup, and raisins.

2 Cut the bananas diagonally into slices, toss them in the lemon juice to prevent them from discoloring, then drain and divide them between 2 individual flameproof dishes.

3 Spoon the rice mixture in an even layer over the bananas so that the dishes are almost full.

4 Sprinkle an even layer of sugar over the rice in each dish.

5 Place the dishes under a preheated moderate broiler and heat until the sugar melts, taking care not to let the sugar burn.

6 Set aside to cool and for the caramel to set, then chill in the refrigerator until ready to serve. Tap the caramel with the back of a spoon to break it.

COOK'S TIP

Canned creamed rice is very versatile and is delicious heated with orange segments and grated apples added. Try it served cold with grated chocolate and mixed chopped nuts stirred through it.

Chocolate Fudge Dessert

This delicious sponge holds a hidden surprise when it is cooked, because it separates to reveal a rich chocolate sauce at the bottom of the dish.

NUTRITIONAL INFORMATION

Calories 397   Sugars 27g
Protein ....10g   Fat 25g
Carbohydrate ...36g   Saturates 5g

10 mins   40 mins

SERVES 4

I N G R E D I E N T S

4 tbsp margarine, plus extra for greasing

6 tbsp light brown sugar

2 eggs, beaten

1½ cups milk

⅛ cup chopped walnuts

⅓ cup all-purpose flour

2 tbsp unsweetened cocoa

confectioners' sugar and unsweetened
   cocoa, for dusting

1 Lightly grease a 4-cup ovenproof dish
   with margarine.

2 Cream together the margarine and
   sugar in a large mixing bowl, until
fluffy. Beat in the eggs.

VARIATION

Add 1–2 tablespoons of
brandy or rum to the mixture
for a slightly alcoholic dessert,
or 1–2 tablespoons of orange
juice for a child-friendly version.

3 Gradually stir the milk into the
   mixture and then add the chopped
walnuts, stirring to mix.

4 Sift the flour and unsweetened cocoa
   into the mixture and fold in gently,
with a metal spoon, until well mixed.

5 Spoon the mixture into the prepared
   dish and cook in a preheated oven,
350°F/180°C, for 35–40 minutes, or until
the sponge is cooked.

6 Dust with sugar and unsweetened
   cocoa and serve.